Speak Your Truth

How You Can Recover from Lupus

Denise A. Dorfman

BALBOA.
PRESS

A DIVISION OF HAY HOUSE

Balboa Press books may be ordered through booksellers or by contacting:

Balboa Press
A Division of Hay House
1663 Liberty Drive
Bloomington, IN 47403
www.balboapress.com
1 (877) 407-4847

Because of the dynamic nature of the Internet, any web addresses or links contained in this book may have changed since publication and may no longer be valid. The views expressed in this work are solely those of the author and do not necessarily reflect the views of the publisher, and the publisher hereby disclaims any responsibility for them.

The author of this book does not dispense medical advice or prescribe the use of any technique as a form of treatment for physical, emotional, or medical problems without the advice of a physician, either directly or indirectly. The intent of the author is only to offer information of a general nature to help you in your quest for emotional and spiritual well-being. In the event you use any of the information in this book for yourself, which is your constitutional right, the author and the publisher assume no responsibility for your actions.

Any people depicted in stock imagery provided by Thinkstock are models, and such images are being used for illustrative purposes only. Certain stock imagery © Thinkstock.

Printed in the United States of America.

ISBN: 978-1-4525-9507-8 (sc)
ISBN: 978-1-4525-9508-5 (hc)
ISBN: 978-1-4525-9509-2 (e)

Library of Congress Control Number: 2014905654

Balboa Press rev. date: 04/10/2014

Contents

Introduction

"Each patient carries his own
doctor inside of him."
—Albert Schweitzer, MD

I remember when I was first diagnosed with lupus. A coworker said to me, "Oh, I am so sorry." I think she thought I was at death's door, that I was not long for this world. I also remember at that instant wanting to say, "No, really, I'm okay. I am not going to die from this illness. Please do not pity me."

I still feel that way. If you are introducing me to someone, please do not introduce me as a person "suffering from lupus," because I don't *suffer* from lupus. I am happy to report that I have no active disease. I consider myself not just a lupus survivor but a lupus thriver. I have successfully sent my disease into remission. I believe lupus can be healed or the course of the illness significantly improved if you are willing to do the mental work necessary to dissolve it. You too can possibly put lupus into remission as I did and have no active disease. It does not matter how life threatening your illness is, or how many symptoms you have, or how many hospitalizations you have had this year. You can heal yourself of this disease or at least greatly improve your quality of life.

I have learned over the years that if we wait for the medical community to come up with a cure, we will have a long wait. I think this illness may be too complicated to be cured with conventional medicine. I believe those of us who are diagnosed with lupus need to go within to make ourselves whole. Even if researchers came up with a drug for lupus that cured most people, it still would not make us whole. A cure is not the same as healing. While a cure will only suppress the symptoms of lupus, healing means to become whole. I believe going within to heal ourselves from lupus is far superior to any drug or surgery that the medical community might come up with.

That being said, I still think conventional medicine has its place in the treatment of lupus. This book is not a substitute for medical care. If you are diagnosed with lupus, get established with a qualified rheumatologist experienced in treating the disease. He or she can prescribe medication to keep you comfortable enough so you can do the mental work needed for healing. To be honest, lupus can be very painful, and you need to find your comfort zone. That's where pain medication and even steroids come in. So please get medical attention. It is necessary to use every modality available on your healing journey.

You may never be "cured" of lupus, but you can be healed. You may still have problems with the disease, but you will feel much better when you do the work outlined in this book.

In this book, I refer to types of lupus with lowercase letters. Hence, you will see lupus, systemic lupus erythematosus (sle), and central nervous system (cns) lupus in lowercase, because I do not want to give this disease any more power or importance by capitalizing the words. This is in keeping with the style of self-help author Louise L. Hay, who referred to aids and hiv with lowercase letters. Also, I do not believe in learning all you can about lupus. I know many people say it's a "good defense." However, I think you are only focusing on the problem, on what you don't want. Focusing on what you don't want only brings you more of it. I believe it is imperative to hone in on the solution, not the problem. Please let your main focus be on healing and wellness, and your body will have the best chance to become well and whole.

Chapter 1

A Primer on the Disease Called Lupus

Symptoms of lupus include joint pain, low white blood count, low red blood count, low platelet count, butterfly-shaped rashes, inflammation of the organs (including the pericardium), muscle pain (due to inflammation), malaise, fatigue, kidney disease, organ failure, Reynaud's syndrome (bluish fingers due to poor circulation), swollen hands, anemia, and generalized inflammation throughout the body.

There is no typical course of lupus; therefore, there is no one-size-fits-all treatment in conventional medicine. Patients can have a case that ranges from mild to life threatening, depending on the symptoms and parts of the body affected. It is an autoimmune disease in which the immune system attacks itself. When a person has lupus, his or her immune system does not know the difference between an antibody and an antigen. An antibody fights infection, and an antigen would increase infection. There is only one medicine that I know of that treats symptoms of lupus: Plaquenil, a quinine-based medication that controls inflammation over the long term. Rheumatologists also prescribe steroids for acute inflammation so the patient can find relief. One of the steroids most commonly used is prednisone, but it can only be used in the short term.

When a doctor is trying to determine if the patient has lupus, he or she will run several blood tests. The first is an antinuclear antibody (ANA) test, which determines whether the antibodies in the patient's body have a nucleus left. When antinuclear antibodies are found in the bloodstream, this indicates that the patient's immune system is attacking itself. Once the test is deemed positive, another one is run to count the number of antinuclear antibodies in the bloodstream. The second test is called the sedimentation rate, or SED rate, which determines the amount of inflammation in the blood. Third, a complete blood count test is ordered. Usually, in someone who has lupus, the white blood count, red blood count and platelet count are low. If all of these tests are positive then the body is trying to fend off disease by the inflammatory response and the immune system using up the white blood cells.

Once diagnosed with lupus, the patient is referred to a rheumatologist. Treatment depends on the symptoms presented. Sometimes the case is mild at first, as mine was, and the rheumatologist will prescribe Plaquenil. If the inflammation and pain become acute, the doctor may prescribe prednisone, cortisone for localized pain, or even narcotics for more generalized pain. However, lupus can be unpredictable. Patients can suddenly wake up with pericarditis (inflammation of the pericardium) or, more seriously, end up with kidney disease. Many lupus patients need to be hospitalized, sometimes for kidney disease, sometimes just for observation if the laboratory tests show very negative results. I have been hospitalized for observation because the lab tests looked bad, even though I felt fine. I've also been on prednisone and narcotics (Percocet) for acute inflammation and pain.

Lupus seems to have a genetic component. Sometimes lupus patients have had a relative with lupus. My great uncle on my father's side, who lived in the early 1900's, may have died from lupus at thirty years of age. At the time no one knew what it was, and there was nothing the doctors could do for him.

There are at least four main types of lupus: systemic lupus erythematosus (sle), central nervous system lupus (cns lupus), discoid lupus, and nephrotic lupus. SLE is fortunately more common and is what I have described above. A more severe type, cns lupus, occurs when the brain and central nervous system are affected. Symptoms of cns lupus include a trifecta of seizures, mental illness, and joint pain. These patients are usually very sick, often have sores all over their bodies, and must be hospitalized. This type of lupus is considered life threatening. (Patients with sle can also have a life-threatening illness if their vital organs, such as the kidneys, are affected. Patients can die when these organs fail, and their function cannot be restored.) The third type, discoid lupus, is basically a skin disease, in which lesions form on the face, scalp, and neck. Seal, the famous singer-songwriter, has discoid lupus, according to A. G. Moore in *A Lupus Handbook: These Are the Faces of Lupus.* He does not seem to suffer from the disease very much, as "he accords it no more importance than he accords any other difficulty he has confronted" (Moore 2011). The final type of lupus is nephrotic lupus, or lupus nephritis, which is simply a serious manifestion of sle, in which the kidneys are affected and renal failure can result (Medscape.com 2012).

Chapter 2

When I First Became Ill

It all started on October 7, 1982. My father had been terminally ill with cancer for about a month. I was devastated. I became severely depressed and psychotic. My mother took me to the hospital, and I ended up in the psychiatric unit. I believe this was my first episode of cns lupus, though that was not my diagnosis at the time. Instead, I was diagnosed with severe depression with psychotic features.

I felt I needed to escape from my father's situation and just gave up on life. I went into my own fantasy world in which I almost believed

I was an infamous religious figure, the Great Whore, from the book of Revelation. I was involved with a fundamentalist group obsessed with the apocalypse. The members were vehemently opposed to abortion, even in cases of rape and incest, and I strongly agreed with them. I had such low self-esteem that I believed I had been raped and had an abortion in the hospital. Ironically, I was a virgin at the time. I was convinced I was terrible, that I was a slut and no good. I even heard voices telling me this. I felt completely separated from God.

I was on a lot of medications, and my mom was very worried about both my dad and me. My father died in December 1982, and I was moved to a different psychiatric hospital where I could go to school. By April 1983 I was better. I hoped I would never have another episode again, because it was one of the most miserable experiences I had ever been through.

After two years without any mental health issues, I went to college at George Mason University. Everything was going well, so my psychiatrist took me off of my medication. That turned out to be a big mistake, because I ended up in the hospital again. This time the diagnosis was schizophrenia since I had had some delusions and visual hallucinations. Now, I think it was simply another episode of cns lupus, though no one really knows what happened to me in those days. I stayed in the hospital for four months and then was transferred to a day treatment program. I stayed with that program for six months and transitioned back into life by working and going to college. I then went to school full time in the fall and winter and worked in the summers. I made sure not to take more than twelve hours of classes at a time in order to reduce stress during my college years. I was on the dean's list several times and graduated with honors.

After college, I got my first job in promotions at an online database company. My job went very well at first. My boss was pleased with my work and gave me a generous raise after only six months of employment. Then I became ill again. This time I had several grand mal seizures, and at times it was also difficult for me to speak. One Saturday I was taken by ambulance to the hospital. No one knew why I had seizures and a manic episode at the same time. Again, I believe it was just another occurrence of cns lupus. My neurologist tried looking at everything, from prescribing MRIs and EEGs to studying my artwork from the time I spent in the psychiatric unit. She found nothing abnormal. I was on a lot of antiseizure medication for many years after this episode because my neurologist was conservative and too afraid that I would have seizures again. I don't think she ever believed me when I told her the seizures had long since stopped because I was also considered mentally ill.

I ended up quitting my job in promotions. It wasn't a good fit for me, and because I was on so much medication, one of which was phenobarbital, I made some mistakes that were rather embarrassing due to impaired judgment.

Finally, for several years, I was doing pretty well with no mental health or seizure issues. I even worked for a defense contractor in a classified environment. When I look back on those days, I feel pretty proud of myself for being able to work in such an environment for as long as I did. I held a top secret clearance and was doing well.

By the time I turned thirty, I had been diagnosed with lupus (sle). I had severe joint pain, and it was difficult to move my fingers. My white blood count, red blood count, and platelet count were low. I ended up in the hospital for observation and was taking Plaquenil for inflammation.

Shortly after being diagnosed with sle lupus, the medication for my mental illness stopped working. I found myself acting strange at work. I was not thinking clearly, and became disoriented. I made several doctor's appointments with my neurologist, rheumatologist, and psychiatrist. My husband took me to the hospital where I stayed in the psychiatric unit. This was the worst episode yet. My rheumatologist considered that I might have cns lupus. However, I did not present its trifecta of symptoms—joint pain, seizures, and mental illness—all at once, so he did not believe I had it. He also could not explain why I was experiencing those symptoms. He did state that I may have had cns lupus in 1982, but no one really knows for sure.

During this last episode, I was suicidal and chose to spend all of my time in the quiet room. I felt safer in a room where the walls were plain white and there was little stimulation. When I looked at mentally healthy people, I was jealous because they seemed to be so happy and have relative inner peace. I particularly remember the moment that became a turning point in my long struggle with my illness. I was sitting in the quiet room, by choice, and decided I wanted to live after all. I couldn't believe what a dope I had been to consider suicide as an option. I then moved to my room and slept. For two weeks I literally would not get out of bed, so the psychiatrist asked my husband to take care of me at home. Also, the insurance was going to run out.

To this day I don't know how my husband took care of me. I was not easy to live with. I often refused to eat or take my medication. However, I did get better and went back to work in that same classified environment. The company was eventually sold, and I was laid off. I never went back to that kind of work again, even though I had a valuable top secret clearance. I felt that the environment only aggravated my illness.

In 1998, I was working for an IT consulting firm as an administrative assistant. I was not doing well there since I was ill much of the time with lupus symptoms. I was quite overweight due to the seizure medication and experienced low-grade fevers and malaise. I went home sick almost every week. I was put on probation and ended up quitting that job. The company was simply not a good fit for me, and my superiors were displeased that I was sick so much. I believe my illness also affected my work performance. I moved on to a much better job at a major oil company in 2000. It was then that my life started to change.

The Road to Wellness

When I was working for the IT consulting company, a coworker introduced me to Mary Kay, a major cosmetics firm based in Dallas, Texas. Even though I did not do very well (I was not the sales type), I did grow a lot in the five years I was with the company.

My unit director introduced me to the world of self-help. I believe that's when I started to heal.She took us to motivational speaking events, and she shared her Nightingale-Conant (motivational) newsletters with me. I also received a lot of loving support from the women in my unit, which contributed to my healing. My self-esteem got better as my unit director praised me to success, which is part of the Mary Kay philosophy. I learned so much as a Mary Kay consultant. I started to read every self-help book I could get my hands on and attracted people who were interested in self-help as well. I learned that there really is no such thing as failure. It is only a mechanism by which we learn to do things right. I discovered this concept in Deepak Chopra's amazing little book, *Creating Affluence*. I still read it every day and feel strongly that it has helped change my consciousness, especially my wealth consciousness. My unit director also taught me that mistakes and failure are how we learn. Therefore, there is nothing to fear in failure as long as we learn from our so-called mistakes. So I wasn't that upset when I found out I was not very good at selling Mary Kay. I had grown so much in those five years that it was well worth the effort.

About one year after I joined Mary Kay, in May 2000, I started working as a customer service representative at the oil company. I was a contractor at first, and the morale in the department was not good. Many employees were unhappy and often complained about their jobs. For some reason, probably due to the inspiration I received as a Mary Kay salesperson, I decided to view this situation more positively. After all, this company had far better managers than I had experienced at the smaller companies where I worked. I felt much better about myself and decided to think for myself. I stood up for myself and told a different story about my work environment. I stopped gossiping, did not allow myself to be influenced, and focused on my work. I felt the managers were actually doing a reasonably good job at running the department. I simply would not participate in the drama everyone else was creating.

One of the main aspects of the job that people really disliked was the fact that everyone was ranked according to their work performance. Many people compared themselves to others and felt they were ranked incorrectly because they were better than someone who ranked higher. I did not participate in this little drama. I refused to compare myself to others, because I was learning that, on a soul level, we are all equal. No one is better or worse than anyone else. I think many people who have lupus feel "less than," that others are more important than them, so they don't speak up or stand up for themselves. I knew enough from reading self-help books that comparing myself to others was a waste of time and energy. I let go of speculating where I ranked. I let management worry about people performing better or worse than others. I refused to obsess about my seriatim ranking, which represented what percentile you were in the department.

Thanks to my positive outlook, my lupus and mental illness symptoms got better. I was rarely sick and actually enjoyed my work. Management noticed my hard work and focus and praised me with positive feedback. I really felt that a large company was the best fit for me. I had finally found the right environment. I started to speak up for myself and to ask for what I wanted at work. I had never felt safe enough to do that at my previous jobs. I decided I wanted to go into billing and asked for the position. Since management liked me, I got the job. That's when I was happiest. I found the job that was the right fit in the right environment. About the same time I discovered Louise Hay and started reading *You Can Heal Your Life*.

The words she wrote in that book just felt right to me. I was already quite intuitive, and this book helped develop my intuition further. I started doing affirmations and meditation daily. I was reading even more self-help books and also started to work out with a personal trainer. I was encouraged to clean up my diet and temporarily dropped refined sugar. My sedimentation rate went back to normal, and my doctor took me off the Plaquenil. He stated, "Whatever you are doing, keep doing it." This is when the doctor declared I had no active disease, and I did not have any mental illness episodes anymore.

Since discovering positive thinking and Hay, I have not had any significant rheumatic, seizure, or mental health events in thirteen years. Yes, I've had minor flare-ups but nothing very serious. When I have these flare-ups, I simply adjust my diet, exercise, and medications and do affirmations. My doctor still thinks I have no active disease because my lab work always looks normal. I believe anyone suffering from lupus does not need to "suffer" anymore. If you can learn to stand up for yourself, ask for what you want, and defend yourself when necessary, you can beat lupus! According to Hay in *You Can Heal Your Life*, the probable cause of lupus is "A giving up. Better to die than to stand up for oneself."

My childhood was happy, even idyllic. However, I was very timid and sensitive. I never learned to defend myself, so I was always picked on. I remember one time in particular when I was riding the bus in middle school and a girl about my age starting picking on me and calling me names. Instead of standing up to her and defending myself, I dealt with it the way I usually did: avoidance. I ended up walking home from school every day. I had to go through woods and cross a creek, which was scary, but not nearly as scary as that bully on the bus. I think I would have rather died than stand up for myself. Later on, at the defense contractor where I worked, I had a "bully" boss who constantly lost her temper with me and abused me. She would often yell at me when I made a mistake. She had difficulty offering constructive feedback because she had her own emotional problems. However, I would not have attracted her into my life if I were not an easy target. After several years of her impossibly high standards and abuse, I finally asked for what I wanted and got a promotion, working for someone else. Unfortunately, I did not initiate the conversation with the director of the department. He took me to lunch and asked me if I wanted to move to a different position. I still could not ask for what I wanted.

It was not until several years later that I asked for what I wanted and stood up for myself. At the oil company, there was a bully who tried to pick on me several times. I finally stood up to her and defended myself, and to my surprise, she simply backed down. I was amazed at how easy it was to stand up for myself. I simply had to state how I felt and say something in my defense. I learned a valuable lesson: most people will just back down when you defend yourself in an assertive, positive way. They also end up respecting you more. The bully from the oil company and I ended up being on very good terms and were friendly with each other from then on. We had worked out our issues, and I finally learned to defend myself once and for all.

Chapter 3

The Lifestyle for Wellness

I believe that when you really feel in your gut that it is easy to stand up for yourself, and you wind up practicing it in your daily life, your lupus symptoms will start to go away. I also believe in the importance of an anti-inflammatory diet. I don't eat red meat very often, and I try to eat meatless meals at least three times a week. Hence, I have very little joint pain. Most of my diet is made up of whole grains, healthy fats, and fruits and vegetables. Some specific foods that have been proven to reduce inflammation are listed below, along with why they reduce inflammation. This information is from the invaluable book *NutriBullet Natural Healing Foods,_*compiled by the makers of the NutriBullet, a nutrition extractor:

- spinach, blueberries, cherries—These foods contain high levels of flavonoids, compounds known to reduce inflammation. They also contain high antioxidant levels.
- avocado, salmon, walnuts—All contain omega-3 fatty acids, which have been shown to disrupt the cell signals that trigger inflammation.
- papaya, pineapple—Both fruits belong to the bromeliad family and contain the enzyme bromelain, which has been shown to reduce inflammatory responses.
- turmeric—Renowned for its anti-inflammatory properties, the spice contains curcumin, a compound known to interfere with chemicals that cause

inflammation. It is helpful both when ingested and when applied topically to skin conditions or injuries.

Inflammation facts

"Inflammation is part of our normal immune response. When the body is harmed, it sends lymph and blood cells through the lymphatic system to flood the area of concern. This fluid uses chemical reactions to separate and remove the harmful substances, restoring the cell back to its normal state.

"While brief periods of inflammation—known as acute inflammation—work to heal the body, inflammation that extends for long periods of time (chronic inflammation) puts a strain on the circulatory and immune systems, damages body tissues, and destroys cells. Chronic inflammation can be attributed to a diet high in processed foods and/or food sensitivities and allergies. Chronic inflammation makes the body more prone to contracting other illnesses and may even cause autoimmune diseases—health problems that occur when the immune system attacks healthy tissues in the body. Autoimmune diseases include celiac disease, cirrhosis of the liver, Crohn's disease, lupus, anemia, psoriasis, arthritis, and type I diabetes among others.

"Eating properly can drastically reduce and reverse chronic inflammation, while eating processed foods cause its development." (Nutribullet Natural Healing Foods 2013)

I have found that when I eat these foods, my joints suffer far less inflammation. Recently, when I bought a nutrition extractor and pulverized combinations of fruits and vegetables, I significantly reduced my morning aches and pains (due to inflammation) within a few days. I highly recommend buying a nutrition extractor and preparing these foods for breakfast. It's such an easy and convenient way to incorporate high amounts of nutritional foods into your diet. It also does not take much time to prepare these foods, since they are raw, and just need to be washed before extraction. You may find, after eating them for several weeks, that you lose a few pounds as well. You will also have more energy, be less hungry, and not crave processed foods as much. I know that when I stopped eating refined sugar, I automatically stopped eating processed foods. I believe that was the key to reduced inflammation. There are several nutrition extractors on the market. These machines can pulverize the seeds and skin of foods as well, so you get the maximum nutrients.

I also believe it is important to get regular, moderate exercise and get plenty of rest every night. Most importantly, I believe you heal yourself on a soul level. You really have to have the inner knowledge that you are worth defending. You also must practice standing up for yourself in your daily interactions. You must love yourself enough to feel you are worth fighting for. You will find that people will not pick on you once they see you defending yourself. They will just do it to someone else, as Hay has often said.

You must also not give up on life, which I feel is another cause of lupus. When my father was terminally ill, I gave up on life and became psychotic. My father had trouble standing up for himself as well. He often was very passive when he and my mother got into arguments. My mother, on the other hand, was strong and formidable. I did not identify with my mother and felt I was much more like my father. When he died, I simply gave up. Thank goodness my mother was strong enough to help me out of my illness. I received so much love and support from her over the years. I also ended up following her example and became a much stronger person.

Occasionally, life will still test me with an opportunity to stand up for myself. Recently, for example, I asked a contractor to do some work on our house. It turned out that the workmen did not do a very good job, and my husband asked them to stop work and leave. I wanted our money back, and they told me "the check was in the mail" twice, but it never showed up. I gave them plenty of time to refund my money. I don't believe in revenge. That usually does not work, because what you give out you get back. However, I don't believe you should let people walk all over you either. I also learned to have compassion for people who try to hurt you. I understood the company was having cash flow problems and could not pay the money back right away. I immediately blessed the situation with love every time I thought about the contractor. I did the best I could to forgive the company for lying to me. It did not take long after that when my refund arrived in the mail.

In *A Lupus Handbook*, Moore cites several instances where she has stood up for herself. For example, she would not accept less than competent medical advice. She consulted several rheumatologists before settling on one who would listen to her and respect her opinions and views. She wanted a doctor she could negotiate with when deciding on her treatment plan. She considers herself "noncompliant"; however, I believe she is simply standing up for herself. I think this characteristic has served her well, as she has had a relatively mild course of lupus and has pretty lengthy periods of good health. Even when I asked her permission to use parts of her book, she stood up for herself and asked for what she wanted. Specifically, she asked me to let her know what parts I was going to use in the book and to run them by her before she gave her consent. She has even checked herself out of the hospital against medical advice when she received incompetent medical care. Her assertiveness is admirable, and I believe that has made her well (Moore 2011).

Another person who has been very successful in coping with lupus is Barbara Enright, whom Moore mentions in her book. Enright won the women's tournament in the World Series of Poker in 1986. Even with her diagnosis, she went on to win several times at the tournament. Below is an excerpt from Moore's profile of Enright, which tells me exactly why she did so well with the disease and probably put it in remission:

"Barbara Enright was born on August 19, 1949, in Los Angeles, California. In her youth she was licensed as a cosmetologist and worked a number of jobs: cocktail waitress, bartender, and stylist for Hollywood celebrities. In the 1970s she tried her hand at poker in the Gardenia, California, card rooms, where she did so well that she eventually quit her other jobs and dedicated herself to poker.

"Barbara asserts that she has never played a 'woman's' game. She comes at her opponents with decidedly 'unfeminine' aggression. Enright explains her success in the traditionally male-dominated poker room: she simply states that she is aggressive and that if a woman is too 'soft' in tournament play, she cannot succeed. But if she asserts herself and defies the expectations of the men sitting at the table with her, she can do 'very well.'"

I believe that Barbara Enright did very well with her disease also, simply because she was assertive and stood up for herself when necessary. Indeed, lupus was simply a "footnote" in her life (Moore 2011). Since her diagnosis, she has lived a very full life, raising a child and managing a successful career. Moore also points out she is "smart, friendly, and focused."

Another woman who has actually put her disease into remission, again mentioned in

Moore's book, is actress Elaine Paige. What I noticed the most about Paige was that she was considered a "difficult" person. I think she was considered difficult because she stood up for herself, especially when it came to the quality of her work. As Moore writes:

"Elaine Paige has a reputation for being a perfectionist—so much so that some have labeled her as 'difficult.' If she is indeed difficult, she is at least as hard on herself as she is on anyone else. Her expectations of herself are very high— she doesn't want just to do well, she wants to do so well that people rise from their seats at the end of a performance and give her a standing ovation.

"She had two bouts of lupus, one in 1989 and one in 1999. Both episodes of lupus went into remission. Let me point out that she promptly sought out appropriate medical care, but I think her 'difficult' personality played a major role in the remission of her disease. It is safe to assume that Elaine Paige stood up for herself when necessary, and did not take any guff from anybody. She also learned from her disease, recognized the symptoms quickly, and got the medical attention she needed. This also demonstrates the healthy respect Elaine had for herself" (Moore 2011).

Many people will probably argue when they read this book that those who stand up and fight can still have severe cases of lupus. My answer to this argument is that these people are probably focusing too much on fighting the disease. They battle it out with lupus. They declare war on the disease. However, this is the wrong focus in my opinion. These individuals are focusing on the problem instead of the solution. Their focus on the disease of lupus will simply create more disease. I think we should focus our efforts instead on standing up for ourselves in all other areas of our lives, and on wellness, and we will create wellness in our lives.

I remember when I was first diagnosed with lupus. For some reason, I did not go out and google the disease and find out as much as I could. I did not even "declare war" on the disease. Intuitively I knew that was the wrong focus. I instead practiced standing up for myself as much as I could and focused on health. I think people, through researching the disease, can become obsessed with this symptom or that symptom. If you are an obsessive type, be obsessed with health, not the disease. I'm not saying that you should be totally ignorant about lupus, but do not pay too much attention to researching possible symptoms or "doing battle" with the disease. I think you will just create more symptoms. I suggest just researching what symptoms you do have, instead of worrying and wondering about what might happen to you. As

I have implied earlier, fear and lupus don't go together well.

I'm also not saying you should give up. That would make your symptoms worse as well. Simply focus on wellness and standing up for yourself in all areas of your life, particularly in finding good medical care, and you should get better. As I have pointed out, lupus simply cannot be active in an assertive person whose focus is on wellness and more meaningful aspects of their lives. Dr. Bernie Siegel would agree with me on this point. He has often said that you should not pay a lot of attention on "fighting" or "waging war" with disease. He makes sure he does not say to his patients that he is going to "kill" the disease (Siegel 2013).

Why I Think There Is No
Cure for Lupus Yet

Lupus is a disease that does not get a lot of attention. Even though more and more people are diagnosed every year, medical science has done little to find a cure, and I believe I know why. Lupus sufferers are not reporting their symptoms every time they arise. Because we have not spoken up for ourselves, symptoms get missed and lupus does not get researched as thoroughly as it could. I think many people don't want to sound like hypochondriacs, or they are sick of being sick and don't want to see the doctor yet again. They don't want to sound silly. I even saw an ad on television imploring people suffering from lupus to report every symptom as it arises. We need to demand that the medical community pay attention to this disease. We need to be more like breast cancer sufferers. We may not have the energy to walk for several days to raise awareness, but we could do a better job of getting the medical community to help find a cure.

I heard recently that there is only one medication approved for lupus, and even that medicine is not appropriate for everyone. Please report any and all symptoms you have to your doctor as soon as you experience them. It is important for the doctor to know everything about your experience with lupus, no matter how subtle or minor the symptom is. It is vital in your recovery. Take care of yourself! That is why I am writing this book—to help others with the disease and raise awareness at the same time.

Exercise: A Safe Way to Stand Up for Yourself

One easy, safe way to stand up for yourself is to ask others for support when you are ill. Tell your friends and family about your disease, and ask for any help that you may need. This is a good beginning point in speaking up for yourself. I once saw a young woman on television who had been hospitalized several times within the year with kidney problems and other lupus-related issues. I was proud of her, because she had taken the first steps in speaking up. She told her friends and coworkers about her disease, and that she was going to participate in the DC Walk sponsored by the Lupus Foundation of America. This was a very positive, important step in her healing. Instead of going to bed, pulling up the covers, and suffering in silence, this young lady asked for what she needed at the time. She was also helping to raise awareness of the disease.

How does it feel to get the support you need when you ask for it? Did you find it easy or difficult to ask for support? Record your responses here:

_____

_____

_____

Exercise

State the following affirmation aloud several times. It is from Hay's book, *You Can Heal Your Life*, and it is the new thought pattern for lupus.

I speak up for myself freely and easily. I claim my own power. I love and approve of myself. I am free and safe.

Pay attention to how you feel when you are saying these words. How does your body react? What emotions come up? Do you feel empowered? Indifferent? Does this new thought pattern feel unfamiliar, strange? Does it feel true for you? Does it seem too simplistic or unrealistic? Any reaction is good; there is no right or wrong response. Record your feelings here.

_____

_____

_____

_____

_____

When I first read the new thought pattern for lupus, it seemed an accurate description of how I was feeling. It was like a bell went off. I thought, "Yes, that's right. That's what I need to think and feel. I need to stand up for myself more often." When I looked at the probable cause of the illness in *You Can Heal Your Life*, which is:

"A giving up. Better to die than to stand up for one's self. Anger and punishment."

All my life, I really did feel that I would rather die than stand up for myself. I avoided confrontation because I could not defend myself. I knew that if I was ever going to overcome lupus, I was going to have to work on loving myself enough to defend myself. I had to feel worthy enough to ask for what I wanted or needed and stand up for my rights. I went to work right away, and it did not take long before I was happier with my life, and I felt better as time went on. This happened only five years after I was diagnosed with sle, and life has gotten better ever since.

Wellness: You Must Feel It

As Wayne Dyer stated in his book *Wishes Fulfilled*, "It is absolutely imperative to learn how to assume, in your imagination, the feeling of already having or being what you desire." Dyer healed himself of leukemia without drugs, chemotherapy, or radiation by doing the following:

> The most important thing I do is choosing to feel good regardless of what the numbers on any medical screen might say. I meditate on I am strong; I am perfect health; and I infuse my entire being, inner and outer, with a feeling of love and gratitude for this moment, this day, this body that has housed my invisible soul for the 71-plus years, and I assume the feeling of the wish fulfilled. I have no thoughts of impending doom, only feelings of love for this miracle that I am. I treat my leukemia diagnosis

as healing information being given to me rather than disease. (Dyer 2012

I couldn't have said it better myself. What if your lupus diagnosis is simply your body's way of getting you to speak up for yourself rather than disease? Also, how would that feel to you, knowing that it was easy to stand up for yourself? How would it feel to be healthy and whole? I believe that once you have the feeling of wellness down pat, your body will respond with perfect health and no active disease—of any kind! That's what happened to me. I affirmed, with the feeling behind it, that I was healthy and whole, and that I easily and freely spoke up for myself. I affirmed it over and over until it became a deep conviction, and before I knew it, I felt better.

Then the lab work "cooperated." However, before the lab work showed normal results, I did not pay attention to the numbers. I let the doctor worry about those abnormal numbers. Here's what I know about lab work that may be useful to you in your healing journey: Lab work is only one test, or set of tests, which describe the state of your body *at one point in time.* It's far more important how you are feeling on a daily basis. Please do not pay too much attention to lab work. Even a doctor will tell you that's it's a snapshot in time. Just pay attention to how you are feeling, and choose to feel good about yourself and your life, and the lab work will follow before you know it.

Forgiveness

It has been said in *A Course in Miracles*, if you have an illness, you need to look around you and see who you need to forgive. I think that forgiving others for perceived injustices was an important step in my healing. I recognized that the bully on the bus in junior high school was in a lot of pain herself. I think she noticed that I was getting attention from the boys at school, and she was envious since she was not getting any attention. She lashed out at me by calling me a "sleaze." She ended up having a lot of other problems. I forgave her for bullying me and felt compassion for her. I set her and myself free from the pain of being picked on.

I also forgave the boss who abused me at the defense contractor where I worked. That was a lot more difficult, because the abuse lasted for about four years. I had a lot of anger and rage and needed to release it. With the help of Hay's anger-releasing tape, I was finally able to let go of the pain she inflicted on me. I also forgave myself for all the times I attacked her. It took several listens of that tape. She was often one of the five people I picked whom I was angry with. When I finally let go of her and the pain, I felt lighter and freer. Now she is free and I am free. Even though I released her from my life a long time ago, I still respect her and feel compassion for her. She too was in pain when I worked for her. She was raised by a mentally ill mother, and I don't think she ever learned to express her emotions properly. Sometimes she would be loving and supportive, and sometimes she would be very cruel. I believe she got this behavior from her mother, who had bipolar disorder. I understand now why she acted the way she did. We are now both free to move on with our lives.

Forgiveness makes you feel better and is good for your mental and physical health. When you can finally let go of past hurts, your cells can respond much better in a more loving environment. Please understand that forgiveness is not condoning the other person's behavior. You are simply deciding not to hold on to the pain anymore. You just let it all go. I believe you can heal much quicker when you are not distracted by perceived wrongs. You are free to think your own loving thoughts. You feel lighter, and you can finally heal.

Loving Yourself

Loving yourself is so important in healing as well. When you forgive yourself and others, you are demonstrating self-love. It is also important to change behaviors that you know deep down are not healthy or right for you, since guilt can erode self-respect. When I decided to stop gossiping, my entire life changed. I was healthier, I received positive feedback at work, and I was respected by others. I decided to take a stand and think for myself. I stopped agonizing over what people thought of me. When I loved myself more, it did not matter what someone said about or did to me. I also was able to defend myself more easily.

Meditation is a wonderful daily practice to find that space of loving yourself. I try to meditate every day by simply breathing deeply and asking for guidance. Meditating also reduces stress and is great for your overall health. When I started enjoying better health, I was meditating every morning.

Chapter 4

My Session with
Dr. Mona Lisa Schulz

Because I was doing so well and had not had any psychiatric episodes since I was thirty, I wanted to know if I should stay on psychotropic medication. I consulted the well-known medical intuitive, Dr. Mona Lisa Schulz, who was very insightful. She was the first person who thought I had cns lupus, that I knew of (my rheumatologist initially thought I might have had cns lupus as well, but later decided I did not have it). She told me to stay on medication, not because I was mentally ill, but because I had symptoms of cns lupus. She did not "see" any mental illness or seizure disorder at all, only lupus, which she saw in every part of my body. Actually, I never felt I had mental illness and was chastised by a psychologist for having "a hard time accepting" that I had it. I've even been accused of denying I had a mental illness. It turns out I may have been right all along.

Dr. Schulz said that my cns lupus started when I was sixteen, when my father was terminally ill with cancer. My father was such a strong influence on me that I was traumatized when I learned he was dying. His opinion of me meant everything to me, and to lose him was like losing a part of my self. Schulz felt that the reason I married an older man was to replace my father. My husband and I have been married for twenty years. It's been a happy, stable marriage. In my defense, I can think of worse ways of coping with the death of a parent. I do not drink, take drugs, and have no addictions at all. Schulz described me as "one of those people doing this stuff." I wasn't sure if she was saying it was wrong or not.

She also advised that I find more fulfilling work to have an outlet besides my marriage. That is when I decided to become a writer. Writing gives me the opportunity to create, using the right side of my brain. I have spent many years using the left side of my brain in repetitive corporate jobs. I always feel great after a session of writing. It's almost like I've given birth, because I have created something. It also feels good knowing that I am helping people in a more meaningful way than at work, where I only resolve billing issues. Since I started writing, I am happier and more satisfied with life. I feel I'm kind of a "situation healer," both in the corporate world and in my writing.

Writing this book is one of my main life purposes. It is my desire that this book will help as many people as possible who are diagnosed with any kind of lupus. But if I can improve even one person's situation with lupus and help him or her thrive, instead of just survive, then I have accomplished something significant and contributed to the light of the world.

A Word about Medication

Many people involved in self-healing would say that medication should be a last resort, if it is used at all. I think medication has its place in your healing, especially when you are having an acute flare-up. Once, when my rheumatologist took me off Plaquenil, I suffered severe pericarditis. The pain was so intense, and it was constant—it did not just hurt when I breathed. My doctor immediately put me on prednisone (a steroid) to reduce the severe inflammation and pain. However, I was on it for only a short period of time and was soon weaned off of it. I think medication is okay, but in minimal amounts, since it can often cause other medical problems.

I understand that Plaquenil is a very safe drug. Many doctors feel it is the lupus patient's "vitamin" since it has almost no side effects and has not been found to cause other illnesses. I am on Plaquenil to this day, but a very low dosage, in order to avoid another acute flare-up. However, I have been off of Plaquenil several times in my life, when I had cleaned up my diet and exercised every day. I think if you stop taking Plaquenil, you must be very careful to reduce stress, exercise every day, and really stick to an anti-inflammatory diet. That can be tough to do on a long-term basis, particularly with the stressful lives we lead.

I am also on ziprasidone for the mental illness symptoms I described earlier. My doctor wanted me to go off of that medicine as well. However, I am reluctant because I lead a stressful life and want to avoid an episode, which I believe now to be a cns lupus flare-up. The episodes I have had were so severe that I was incapacitated and required inpatient hospitalization. Since these episodes can alter my life so much, I would rather stay on the lowest effective dose of ziprasidone. I do notice that I tolerate this medication very well. I do not have the weight gain, high cholesterol, and arrhythmia that can happen with ziprasidone use. I have only had some mild dizziness when I am in a very warm environment. I feel fortunate that I have found an effective medication that I can tolerate so well. However, I'm not sure if it is doing anything to prevent mental illness at this point since I have not had an episode in seventeen years. I used to have an episode every few years even on medication, so it appears that the mental illness is truly in remission.

Exercise: Using Your Subconscious Mind for Healing

This exercise has been adapted from Dyer's *Wishes Fulfilled*. He states that you can manifest anything, including healing, by "programming" wellness into your subconscious.

Write this on an index card and place it by your bed: I am going to use these moments to review what I intend to manifest into my life.

Repeat at least three times this quote from Saint Germaine in the "I AM" Discourses: "I AM" the Governing Presence, governing in Perfect Divine Order, commanding Harmony, Happiness and the Presence of God's Opulence in my mind, my home, and my world.

Feel the sustaining power of this in your body.

In the last five minutes before you drift off to sleep, program your subconscious mind for wellness. Try to replicate how it feels in your body to be healthy and whole. Imagine and experience your body as pain free. How does it feel to be energetic and active? You may want to go back to the time before you were diagnosed with lupus. What activities would you participate in if you were well again? Would you exercise more? Would you do more during the day? Really try to get a sense of how that state feels in your body.

According to Dyer, your subconscious mind is responsible for 96 percent of what you do on a daily basis, and you can manifest every desire you have through your subconscious mind. You only need to program it with your conscious mind. You access your subconscious mind every night while you sleep, and it will eventually, over time, influence your waking state if you consistently practice this every night.

I have created wellness with a similar exercise whenever I've had acute flare-ups, and I have been amazed when even pericarditis would disappear by the next morning and I could go to work the next day. When I was experiencing this very painful condition in my chest at night, before I fell asleep, I simply told myself that I was healthy and whole. I imagined my chest as being pain free. I imagined going to work the next day feeling well. Those thoughts were programmed into my subconscious mind when I went into my dream state. I was delighted to wake up the next morning feeling well enough to go to work. I was also pleasantly surprised. I was not really aware at the time that I was programming wellness into my subconscious mind. According to Dyer, "remember that the last thought you have in your mind can last up to four hours in the subconscious mind. That's four hours of programming from just one moment of contemplation prior to going into your unconscious state."

Be sure to do this every night if possible. It can really help with your overall healing of lupus or, like me, can come in handy during acute flare-ups. I also think if you dream of wellness and you remember that dream, then you really know you have programmed your subconscious mind. By the way, this technique can be used to fulfill any desire. I have been trying to increase my prosperity and was delighted to actually dream of having a million dollars in the bank to buy a sports car!

Why I Believe Most Lupus Patients Are Women

Many people diagnosed with lupus are young women around the age of thirty. I believe most lupus sufferers are women because lupus is a disease caused by not standing up for yourself. Women are socialized in western society that it is not feminine or nice to speak up for themselves. I even saw an article in a magazine recently with the title: "How to Stand Up for Yourself (in the Nicest Way Possible." I believe that illustrates how women are taught to defend themselves.

They must do it in the mildest manner possible, or they will be considered bitchy or aggressive. It's no wonder that so many young women are plagued with lupus. This has certainly been an issue with me since childhood, and I believe many other lupus sufferers have the same issue.

I think society needs to encourage women to be more like the Celtic goddess Brigit, who always stated, "Stand up for what you believe is right." Brigit is a good archetype for any lupus sufferer. Doreen Virtue, in her great Goddess Guidance Oracle cards, provides the following message from the goddess Brigit:

First, be quite clear about your intentions. If you're unclear, then confusion will lessen your power and force. Like a candle in the dark, be very clear and bright in what is acceptable to you in this situation. Make no mistake: I will guide and protect you. And yet, think if the unparalleled rise in your own viewpoint if you are to stand up for yourself, and speak about your needs and your deepest truth! Now is the time to touch your power, for its heat and flame will ignite your passion, which will propel you forward in countless ways. Even in the face of fear, you can still stand up for your ideals and your truth. Be unwavering, and make your stand today!

Brigit couldn't have been clearer: it's imperative that we stand up for ourselves, or our needs will be left behind, and we will continue to suffer. As I've stated before, lupus can be rendered inactive by standing up for yourself more and more until it becomes a habit.

How to Manifest Wellness

I learned to manifest wellness using the same principles I use to fulfill any desire. For example,

I decided I wanted a white leather purse from a major designer. It cost $498, and I had a coupon for 25 percent off. However, I was not making much money at the time, and I could not justify even paying $373.50 for this purse. So I put the desire out there in the universe and waited for any opportunities.

Soon I had an opportunity to repair an old purse that was given to me. I took it into the shop for repairs, and it turned out the old purse was irreparable. However, they gave me a coupon for 40 percent off any new item in the store! Also, I found out that I was going to inherit some money from a relative who had passed several years ago. Suddenly, it was possible to buy that white leather purse I desired! It was only $298 with the coupon, and I felt that was an acceptable price for a handbag.

I had the desire to purchase that white leather bag, put my attention on it, released the desire to the universe, and then looked for opportunities and guidance. It is very important that you release your attachment to the outcome, because then opportunities to manifest your desire will happen sooner than you think.

I also manifested a job in much the same way. My husband was very ill, and I had to spend a lot of time away from work to take care of him. Because it was a temporary assignment and I was a contractor, I lost the job due to my frequent absenteeism. I was disappointed but knew deep down that I needed to be there for my husband at that time. Fortunately, I was able to collect unemployment and borrow from our savings for income. At that time, I purchased *Getting into the Vortex*, a very effective CD by Esther and Jerry Hicks, to help release any resistance to financial abundance. For about four months, I did what I needed to do for my husband, and he got better. I saw an ad on the Internet for a job at a major cable company in billing. I felt I was a good fit for it and had a good feeling about applying. I believe because I had the desire to work for that company in that job, and since I did the work to release the resistant thoughts, results came quickly. Within a week or so after applying, I got an interview with the recruiter and then an interview the next day with the hiring manager, with whom I got along very well. She stated how impressed she was with me, and the next day I received an offer at the salary I wanted. That was the quickest "job manifestation" I had ever had!

It's the same when you manifest wellness. I still occasionally get flare-ups even though my disease is not active. I would get pericarditis occasionally, and it would interfere with daily activities if I did not manifest wellness and send it packing. First, I do take a mild pain reliever to get to the mental place where I can focus on wellness. I think it's perfectly fine to use medicine in order to be able to concentrate on getting well. Second, I take a short walk before bedtime to get myself more centered and calm. Third, I climb into bed and repeat this "itis" affirmation over and over five minutes before I fall asleep: My thinking is peaceful, calm, and centered. I also do a heart affirmation: My heart beats to the rhythm of love and joy. I lovingly allow joy to flow through my mind and body and experience. These affirmations were taken from Hay's *You Can Heal Your Life*. I then make sure I sleep at least eight to ten hours to get the rest my body needs to repair itself.

Often it only takes one evening of doing this process and I experience significant relief. I am able to go about my daily activities the next day. However, you can repeat this process if you are still experiencing any kind of inflammation. I highly recommend using Hay's_*You Can Heal Your Life* or *Heal Your Body* as a reference for any "itis" you experience in any part of the body.

I believe in order to manifest wellness, you must use intuition and logic together. I agree with Hay and Schulz who state in their wonderful book *All is Well*:

> If we are to fully heal, we must bring our attention to the messages our bodies relay through intuition. But we also need logic and facts to fully understand which imbalances in our lifestyle are affecting our health. Just like needing both tires inflated on a bicycle, you need to balance emotions and intuition with logic and fact. Both extreme logic without intuition and intuition without logic breed disaster. We must use both of these tools to create health.

This is why I feel that certain lifestyle changes are as essential as intuition to recover from lupus. Diet, exercise, and rest are so important when you are recovering from this disease. It's imperative that you give up or at least significantly reduce foods that can increase inflammation in the body. These foods include animal products, especially meat. I think one of the best diets for people with lupus is the Mediterranean diet, or Andrew Weil's wonderful anti-inflammatory diet. These diets don't include a lot of meat and animal products, which can aggravate joint pain and other "itis" conditions in the body.

Vigorous exercise is extremely important. My rheumatologist of many years thought exercise was the closest thing to a magic bullet there was in maintaining wellness. When I was working out most days of the week with a personal trainer, I was not only in the best physical shape of my life, but also all of my lab work was perfect. I was doing so well that the doctor took me off Plaquenil. I felt terrific as well.

I don't think there's any substitute for regular exercise. I must admit that I struggle to find the time to fit it in, but one of my goals is to make it a priority in my life like I did before. Lately I have been exercising in the early morning. That way it is done before I even start my workday. That may work for you as well. My rheumatologist suggested that a good way to get your exercise is to schedule it—put it in your calendar as an appointment. I understand you can always ask your guides or your angels to help you fit it into your life.

One caveat is to always consider impact. You must protect your joints, or you will end up getting your knees replaced as you get older. You also may end up with back and hip problems later in life if you are not careful with your joints. Please keep this possibility in mind if you are considering running marathons or any other high-impact exercise. You could end up paying for it down the road, and I know from personal experience it's not fun. My husband has lower back pain and has had both knees replaced. His back and knees went out on him because he was so active in running and sports as a younger man.

Rest is the third lifestyle consideration. I think you need eight hours of sleep a night at the minimum. We all lead such stressful, activity-filled lives that our bodies need to restore themselves every night. I believe if we are ill, or even just experiencing a flare-up, we need nine or ten hours of sleep at night. I know when I'm experiencing a flare-up, sleeping ten hours at night seems to help clear up whatever "itis" I have. My doctor agrees that rest does help, especially with pericarditis. Rest gives your body a chance to heal.

I had an episode recently in which my arms were so arthritic I felt as if they were going to fall off. I was in so much pain, and it came and went until both arms were on fire. I lay in bed thinking about how to handle this pain; it was difficult to sleep. Then I pulled out Hay's great little blue book, *Heal Your Body.* I looked up arms and found this affirmation: I lovingly hold and embrace my experiences with ease and with joy.

I learned that the arms represent the capacity and ability to hold the experiences in life. I simply repeated the affirmation silently over and over. I did this about thirty times. I even acted out the affirmation by holding my pillow, which to me represented my experiences. The pain went away and never came back! I was able to go back to sleep and slept soundly for the rest of the night.

I'm always amazed at how affirmations can relieve minor flare-ups so quickly. I did not have to go to the medicine cabinet and take naproxen; I only had to release the probable cause. You can look up an affirmation either by the disease or condition, or you can go to the body part that is affected. You will know intuitively which one is right for your particular situation. The affirmation will just feel right to you.

That evening, I was fretting about a dream I had about my father. In the dream, he was smiling and then crying. I was wondering why he was crying. I concluded that he was shedding tears for my life situation. Specifically, my husband was in ill health and in a wheelchair, and my mother was in an assisted-living facility for dementia. I was feeling pretty sorry for myself. I was not embracing my experiences well. I was thinking about how confused my mother got sometimes, and I had recently experienced that when I visited her. I also lamented about my husband's immobility, even though he was trying to walk again. That night, when I repeated that affirmation, I released the negative feelings I was having about my recent experiences. That is why the burning arthritis cleared up so quickly.

Another probable cause of lupus is not taking enough care of yourself while taking care of others. Other people always come first, and lupus patients do not stand up for themselves. In *All is Well*, Hay and Schulz describe a case study in which an individual named Andrea took care of her brothers and sisters while even sacrificing her own safety. Eventually, Andrea was diagnosed with sle. Schulz used conventional medicine for the inflammation, as well as Chinese herbs. Also, she gave Andrea specific affirmations for lupus to repeat over and over, for instance: I speak up for myself freely and easily. I claim my power. I love and approve of myself. I am free and safe. Andrea also suffered from scoliosis and joint pain, and she was given specific affirmations for those illnesses as well.

In *All is Well*, Schulz states that lupus lies in the first emotional center of the body, which deals with safety and security. She writes:

> The health of the first emotional center depends on your feeling safe in the world. If you don't have the support of family and friends that you need to thrive, you

will see the insecurity manifest in your blood, immune system, bones, joints, and skin. The key to enjoying health in this center is balancing your own needs with those of the meaningful social groups in your life. Family and friends, work, and an organization to which you are devoted all take up time and energy. But they are also meant to give back, in the form of friendship, safety, and security; they should provide a sense of belonging. These are all reasons human beings seek out other people and groups. However, the needs of the group should never be allowed to overshadow your own needs— particularly your health.

I, too, had a situation recently where it was very easy to put others' needs before my own. In 2011, my husband and my mother both were ill. At first, my husband's kidneys were failing; that was followed by pneumonia and other infections. He was in and out of the hospital several times that year, and he almost died twice. At the same time, my mother became ill with diverticulosis. She also had to go into assisted living. She could no longer live independently or drive. Thank goodness I had the support of family and friends during this time. I know how easy it is to not take care of yourself while taking care of loved ones. There were times when I would forget to take my medicine or take a shower because I was so busy taking care of family. I was fortunate though. I made a conscious effort to care for myself as much as I could before it was too late. Luckily, I never came down with lupus symptoms and was able to take care of my family. I believe if I had not felt supported, and had put others above myself on a consistent basis, I would have gotten ill again with lupus. I think I had gotten to the place where I loved myself enough to care for myself.

I don't know what I would have done without my mother's good friends, who helped move her things out of her condominium and into the assisted living facility. They really made things easier for me since I had so much going on at that time. I only had to worry about selling the condo.

As Hay has often said, all disease, as well as any other problem in life, basically comes from not loving yourself. If I had not loved myself enough to care for myself, I would have not stayed healthy or even found the great job I have at the cable company. At the perfect time, life moved me to the new job quickly and easily. I feel so grateful to Hay for starting her publishing house. If it weren't for her and other Hay House authors mentioned in this book, I would not be as happy and healthy as I am now. Thank goodness these wonderful authors gave me the tools to heal even lupus.

Your immune system's function is to defend the body against disease. When you don't stand up for yourself, when you put others' needs before your own, you are not defending yourself. In turn, the body responds by creating the disease lupus.

I'm sure many people with lupus who read these words may think, "Wait a minute—I stand up for myself plenty, and I have lupus! What gives?" I think it may be because you are not speaking up for yourself in some area of your life, usually a major one. For example, I know of a person with lupus who lives a "biker" lifestyle. Her husband is part of a motorcycle gang. Now, to many people, she seems pretty assertive. After all, she's a biker chick, right? I took a closer look at this woman's lifestyle. Evidently, her husband has made a lot of enemies over the years. Therefore, their personal safety is compromised every day. This woman would never speak up and say that she does not feel safe, because it would mean she and her husband would have to leave the life he loves. So she has become complacent. I suggest that this has made her lupus worse. Her sense of safety being compromised has adversely affected her first emotional center, which is the immune system. I believe that is why her lupus is so severe. I also believe she would be in much better health if her husband quit this biker lifestyle.

Here are some probing questions that may help you hone in on why you have lupus, or somehow unwittingly have made it worse over time.

Do you often put others' needs before your own? If you are doing this, you are saying to the universe that you are not worth defending, that you are worthless.

Do you feel less important than others? If you feel less important than others, you do not feel important enough to take care of yourself. The truth is, you are equal to others. No one is more important than you are, and you are not more important than others.

Was it hard for you to defend yourself in the past? When someone bullied you as a child, did you not have the courage to stand up for yourself? Or did you just try to ignore it and avoid the bully growing up? That is what happened to me throughout my childhood. That is how I made the connection between not standing up for myself and the onset of lupus.

Do you, or did you in the past, sacrifice your personal safety for others? Like the example with the biker's wife and Schulz's patient, people with lupus really hurt their immune systems by putting their personal safety at risk.

Do you ever feel like giving up? Do you give up too easily? To the extent that Moore felt like giving up, her lupus only became worse. It was not until she decided to not give up that she found the right doctor who listened to her and respected her. Of course, she got healthier when she stopped giving up.

These questions may help you figure out where your case of lupus may have come from. If you sit down in a quiet place, center yourself, and ask these questions, you just may find out where you are not "speaking your truth." Also look at times in your life when your illness got better and when it got worse, and try to determine what was going on in your life at those times. Your own assessment of what went on could be the key to figuring out why you have lupus in the first place.

Chapter 5

Why I Suffered for Fourteen Years

Looking back on that period in my life when I was so ill, I came to the conclusion that it was all necessary in my healing journey. I created mental illness and seizures because I was running away from life. According to Hay in *Heal Your Body*, both psychiatric illness and seizures represent escapism, running away from family and from life. During those turbulent years, I was not very happy most of the time. At least at first, I was not in a stable relationship, could not decide on a career, and was generally unsettled in life. I had very poor self-esteem. I could not recognize my physical beauty, let alone my talents and abilities. No wonder I wanted to run away. I also wanted to get away from my mother, which was normal and natural for my age.

When I read the probable causes for seizures and mental illness in Hay's book, it really resonated with me. I started to repeat the affirmation for psychiatric illness: This mind knows its true identity and is a creative point for divine self-expression. (Hay 1999) At this time, I was learning to express myself and, of course, speak up for myself and ask for what I wanted in life. When I was ill, I didn't know what I wanted. That suffering taught me many valuable lessons. I would not want to go through it again. Mental illness is miserable, and my episodes were severe. Even my seizures were severe. However, I'm glad I did go through it because of the many things I learned. I feel better about myself, and I no longer criticize myself. I am also learning not to judge others. I am finding that criticizing others is just as unpleasant as criticizing myself. It's unnecessary and a waste of time and energy. I settled on a career I enjoy and have been happily married for twenty years. Even most of my money problems have cleared up in the time I have gotten well. I have found that when one area of your life comes together and heals, the other areas follow. Even my body weight normalized after I stopped taking all of the medicines I was on! I have stayed at a normal weight ever since my doctor told me how well I was doing and that I had no active disease. It's said that hindsight is twenty-twenty. I can see so clearly now why I went through all of those episodes. You are on a similar pathway. The illness you are suffering from is important in your growth. It is my desire that you will discover why it was necessary after you get better as well.

The Importance of a Nurturing Rheumatologist

Dr. Lissa Rankin, in her innovative book, *Mind over Medicine*, emphasizes the importance of choosing a doctor who cares. She cites an example from a Harvard medical study where "the [positive] response to a placebo increased from 44 percent to 62 percent when the doctor treated the patient with 'warmth, attention and confidence'. Among a third control group of people on a waiting list who received no medical care at all, only 28 percent improved."

She goes on to say it is important that the doctor is optimistic and believes in the treatment he is giving you. She cites a study conducted by the National Institute of Mental Health, in which researchers found that "if a doctor believed that a patient would improve, he or she was more likely to do so than if the doctor did not radiate this type of positivity." (Rankin 2013)

I found this to be true with my rheumatologist as well. He often demonstrated that he cared by not rushing through the appointment and by asking probing questions that got into the details of my lifestyle and general well-being. For example, he was a great believer in exercise and would always ask me if I was exercising, and if I was, what I was doing specifically for exercise. He felt that it was extremely effective in any rheumatic disease, and he wanted all of his patients to exercise. He asked me at one point if I was happy and would note in my record if I was teary that day. He even, at the beginning of the appointment, made small talk about how I was doing in my life. When I got better and he declared that I had no active disease, he stated, "I wish I could take the credit for this turnaround, but I really can't." However, I believe his nurturing and optimistic bedside manner did contribute to my newfound wellness, as the aforementioned studies support.

A nurturing doctor who cares is important, but it's also important for a lupus patient to have a support network in place, one in which he or she feels loved and cared for by family and friends. Also, if you find that you do all the right things—affirmations, exercising, eating right— and have a supportive network of doctors, family, and friends, and you are still showing signs of active lupus, take a look at what else is going on in your life. Is your job stressful? Do you feel valued at work? Are you being bullied at work by your supervisor or coworkers? Are your finances a mess? Do you have "more month than money" and you're trying to make ends meet? All of these negative aspects of your life can produce what Rankin calls stress responses in your physical body, which produce disease as well.

You may find in your healing journey that your job is making you sick, and you may have to switch jobs or quit altogether so you can concentrate on your self-care and healing. That's precisely what I did. I left my stressful job at the defense contractor in that classified environment, and found a far less stressful job where people were kinder to me and generally more professional. I also was not in an environment where my integrity was scrutinized every day. That's what triggered my biggest stress response. Yes, I had a top secret clearance, but I felt like I was in a fish bowl and my integrity was always under a microscope. That could be another issue in a job. You may not be in a classified environment, but you may be selling out by doing something that goes against your values and sense of integrity. That to me is the number one stressor. The defense contractor also was engaged in making products that were used in warfare, and that was hard for me to swallow. Perhaps you work for a company that makes weapons or products in which you don't believe. Or it could be subtler, where the salespeople are dishonest or the customer service is shoddy, and you feel guilt by association and don't want to be a part of that company.

You may also need to take steps to improve your finances, as financial wealth has been shown to be linked to better health, and poverty has been linked to increased disease (Rankin 2013). I won't go into too much detail about finances—that's a subject for a whole other book—but know that there are self-help resources out there that can help you improve your finances. I find that tithing can be effective in improving your finances. However, you must give with the highest intention: you are returning to a higher power with gratitude for all he/she has given to you to contribute to the light of the world. When I started to tithe, little financial miracles started to show up in my life. Premium parking places would appear out nowhere (and not a handicapped space!). I applied for a credit card and was approved with no interest for fifteen months and a $200 signing bonus. I received an expensive item free that I ordered for all the shipping trouble I went through with a particular retailer. I even got "unexplained" credits showing up on my credit card statement, for which there did not seem to be a rational explanation.

People Who Experience Spontaneous Remission—Three Things in Common

According to Dr. Joan Borysenko, people who are lucky enough to experience a spontaneous remission have three things in common. Note: This does not necessarily mean that you will experience a remission if all of these things are present in your life. This is simply what the research has found in these individuals:

1) A belief in human potential—that it is possible for human beings to heal themselves of illness

2) A belief in their own potential—that it is possible for them to heal themselves

3) They experience a spiritual transformation. (Borysenko 2013)

Though the remission in my case was not exactly spontaneous, it did happen relatively quickly (in a few years) after I discovered I had lupus and started my spiritual journey. At that time, I did start to believe that the body knew how to heal itself. I had heard many stories of people whose cancer went into remission. I also believed very strongly that I, too, could get better. It took a while, but I did go through a spiritual transformation, though it was not dramatic. I became less angry and more grateful. I stopped gossiping and judging myself and others. I learned to love myself and appreciate others and the beauty surrounding me. I started to keep a gratitude journal, where I listed at least five things to appreciate each morning. I forgave others for perceived wrongs in the past and present.

I think these last two practices are extremely important when one is ill. Gratitude not only helps you see what is going right in your life, no matter how sick you are, but also brings more to be grateful about. And, as it is often quoted from *A Course in Miracles*, "When you are ill, look around and see who it is you need to forgive." Forgiveness and gratitude are the spiritual magic bullets and can be transformative when practiced.

Chapter 6

Conclusion

It is my desire that as you are healing, you focus on creating wellness in your body and your life. As I have stated before, don't think of yourself as "battling" the disease of lupus. If you do that, you will only create more of the disease. Focus on optimal health and I believe you will be healed, or at least substantially improve your life situation.

Second, the main key to healing yourself of lupus is to remember to stand up for yourself. Affirm that it is easy to stand up for yourself and repeat that often. Love and respect yourself enough to defend yourself and ask for what you want from others. Remember, you are not any less important than anyone else, nor more important. Keep in mind that you count and you are equal to others.

Third, avoid inflammation-causing foods and include anti-inflammatory foods in your diet. Freshly extracted anti-inflammatory fruits, vegetables, nuts, and seeds are always great for you. Get at least eight hours of sleep every night, and exercise when you can.

Fourth, choose a compassionate and competent doctor who is optimistic and values your opinions and beliefs. It's your way of saying to the universe, "I love and respect myself enough to seek out the best care I can find."

Finally, start to forgive others for any perceived wrongs. It also is a sign of self-love and self-respect. Remember that forgiveness is just letting go of the pain that this person or persons caused you. It has nothing to do with the other person—it is only about you.

It is my desire for you to fully recover from lupus as I did and suffer no more. It is my wish that this book be an important resource in your journey of self-healing. I send my love and best wishes to you as you heal from this disease and live a happier, healthier, more productive life. I support your growth. God bless you all!

References

Beck, M. 2013 "How to Stand Up for Yourself (in the Nicest Way Possible)." O Magazine, July

Borysenko, Joan. 2013 "The Art of Healing." Hay House World Summit, June

Chopra, Deepak. 1993 *Creating Affluence.* Amber-Allen Publishing, San Rafael, CA.

Dyer, Wayne. 2012*Wishes Fulfilled: Mastering the Art of Manifesting*. Hay House Publishing, Inc.,

Foundation for Inner Peace. 1992 *A Course in Miracles*. Mill Valley, CA

Hay, Louise L. 1989 "Anger Releasing." Audiotape. Carson, CA

-*Heal Your Body* 1982 Hay House Publishing, Inc., Carlsbad, CA

-. *You Can Heal Your Life* 1999 Hay House Publishing, Inc., Carlsbad, CA

Hay, Louise L., and Mona Lisa Schulz. 2013 *All is Well* Hay House Publishing, Inc., Carlsbad, CA

Hicks, Esther, and Jerry Hicks 2010 *Getting into the Vortex*. CD. Hay House Publishing, Inc., Carlsbad, CA

NutriBullet Natural Healing Foods 2013 Homeland Housewares, LLC

Moore, A. G. 2011 *A Lupus Handbook: These Are the Faces of Lupus* Westbury, NY

Rankin, Lissa 2013 *Mind Over Medicine* Hay House Publishing, Inc., Carlsbad, CA

Siegel, Bernie 2013 "The Art of Healing," Hay House World Summit, June

http://emedicine.medscape.com/article/330369-overview Medscape.com

http://www.webmd.com/a-to-z-guides/chronic-kidney-disease-treatment-overview

WebMD.com

http://www.kidney.niddk.nih.gov/kudiseases/pubs/lupusnephritis/ NIH.gov